Plymstock in Perspective

Arthur L. Clamp

The tower of Plymstock church seen beyond the trees
from a point in Church Road around 1900.

This version of the book is virtually as originally published.
There are now additional pages at the back providing information about the author.

The republishing project is being managed by Arthur's grandson, Steven Gibson. We aim to find all the research that he was involved in publishing, preserving it for the next generation as part of 'The Clamp Collection'.

INTRODUCTION

THIS pictorial excursion into the changes of the past few decades is intended primarily to be one of recording scenes, people and places which have almost disappeared through the building developments since the 1950s. It has not been set out to cover, in any order, all these changes or to aspire to being a comprehensive account of the one time rural community of Plymstock which many of its senior citizens can still remember. Its purpose is rather to remind old and young alike of features of the locality which contributed towards its make up. The title *Plymstock in Perspective* sums this up.

The Plymstock area bordering the coastline and Laira, and with its northern acres rubbing shoulders with Plympton parish, has been farmed and lived upon for many hundreds of years. Its church tower has over watched the former fields and farms for a similar period of time and many of Plymstock's sons went to sea or found employment in a wide range of local work and, of more recent years, sought their fortune in Plymouth, the Dockyard, or went "up the line". Their imprint on the locality has gone but careful searching of trade directories will soon reveal quite an astonishing range of activities. There were quarrymen, lime burners, farmers, farriers, market gardeners, butchers, bakers, grocers, shoe makers, tailors, painters, millers, stone masons and many others who found employment in the parish. Plymstock also had its fair share of "gentry", that is well to do families which contributed in a variety of ways to the running of the village. Of these perhaps the Harris's of Radford House made the most lasting impression on Plymstock but they have gone as well as their fine mansion down at Radford.

One should not, however, bemoan too much over these changes. Transport and communications by rail, road and sea have brought in new ideas and people with needs for housing, schools, shops and services. The heart of the village has become the heart of a large area of housing estates giving good access to Plymouth and a favourable locality for bringing up a family. The small village shops have been replaced by the supermarket; the Broadway is a mecca for shoppers for miles around. Garages have developed to service cars, doctors' group practices to exercise medical care over a growing community, national buses have replaced the locally-owned operators and we all take for granted being "on the mains", having gas and electricity and linked by phone to thousands of subscribers.

This was certainly not the picture of just a few decades ago. Electricity came to Plymstock in 1928, water to houses was laid on around the time of the First World War, cess pits were quite common up to the Second World War and buses and cars had to pay to cross Laira "iron" bridge up to 1924.

Two land sales influenced the pattern of ownership in Plymstock and partly contributed towards the developments which have so altered the old village. The Duke of Bedford was the principal landowner for hundreds of years but decided in 1911 to dispose of various estates throughout the land including that of Plymstock. A very substantial sale of farms, buildings and land attracted enormous attention and resulted in possibly the greatest shift in ownership ever seen in the area. The Radford estate, owned by the Bulteel family, was sold in 1914 with similar results. The house went to the Mitchells of Pomphlett although they did not live in it. The majority of houses in the area are owner-occupier and reflect the aspirations of families of having "a place of their own" something which was the exception not too many years back.

The map in this booklet will show the extent of the old village at the time of the First World War and the various open fields which are now almost all gone. Look at this carefully and the well, farms, few residential houses, narrow lanes, etc. contrast with the density of buildings and numerous roads that form Plymstock today. Many of the older buildings still stand but have been put to other uses.

I am indebted to a number of people for their help in preparing the material for this title. Mr. R. Glinn, of Liskeard, Dr. Noy Scott, of Yelverton, Mrs. Crocker, of Looe, Mr. F. Rowland, of Wembury and Mr. H. Triggs must be mentioned among others who kindly made suggestions and offered advice. I still have more photographs than shown in this book and would be pleased to have the loans of any others, together with anecdotes of the village life, which could possibly form a part II of *Plymstock in Perspective*.

October, 1982.

Arthur L. Clamp,
203 Elburton Road,
Plymstock, Plymouth, Devon.

Pomphlett Sunday School, 1957

The young boys of the school are obviously well turned out for the occasion of the anniversary in 1957 with buttonholes as well. The wearing of a small flower was a custom for years in the Plymstock area on these annual occasions. The twins, Matthew and Edward Campbell, David Rogers and Phillip Martin have been identified but unfortunately no others so far.

Pomphlett Methodist Church Sisterhood Outing in 1955

Annual outings are always part of the calendar of events for various sisterhoods in the churches. This one went to Gwennap pit in Cornwall and seen here are Mr. and Mrs. Beale, Mr. and Mrs. Watts, Mr. and Mrs. Tozer, Mr. and Mrs. Davis, Mr. and Mrs. Symons, Mrs. Dyer, Mrs. Phillips, Mrs. Larkworthy, Mrs. Northcott, Mrs. Axworthy, Mrs. Trinnaman, Mrs. Mytton, Mrs. Horton and Mrs. Wyatt.

Wartime in Plymstock

The Plymstock Rescue Squad, Civil Defence and Ambulance Drivers assistants at Plymstock School in 1943. Joan Thorpe, Olive Lewis, Hilda Deld, Nellie Williams, Roma Shillabeer, Dick Dent, Jim Redding, Charlie Ciniam, Jim Simmonds, Sid Damerell, Dennis Reid, Lottie Toms, Charles Hollewell, T. Barnes, George Crocker, Mrs. Noy Scott, Dr. Noy Scott, Don Oxland, Mrs. Nelder, Jenkin Thomas, George Weeks, Sid Saunders, W. Skelly, Miss Nelder, Claud Lovell, Gwyn Parcell, Marion Rowland, Colin Passmore, D. H. Davey, Betty Acland, Edna Oliver and others. Members are assembled below before uniforms were issued.

Brailey's Smithy at Staddiscombe

Frederick Brailey at work at Staddiscombe for the then important daily task of shoeing local farm horses. He later moved to the smithy at Plymstock taking over from Mr. Mumford. Sam Horn, of Pomphlett, is holding the other horse. The photograph was taken around 1920.

Village Pump and Trough

This stood almost opposite Amberley House close to Hollin's Well from which it drew its water. It was certainly used for drinking by passing horses and would have probably been used at any earlier time for obtaining water for domestic use. Nothing remains of either water supply.

Anglican Mission Church

The interior view of this small mission church which was burnt down at Staddiscombe in the 1920s.

Plymstock,

With the villages of ORESTON, TURNCHAPEL, HOOE, ELBURTON, POMPHLET, BILLACOMBE AND STADDISCOMBE, is a parish and large straggling village, situated in a pleasant valley, near Cattewater Harbour and Plymouth Sound, two miles E. by S. from Plymouth. It is in the Plympton St. Mary union, East Stonehouse county court district, Plympton hundred and Rural Deanery, Totnes archdeaconry and Parliamentary division. The church, dedicated to St. Mary and All Saints', is a large edifice, in the Perpendicular style, with a tower containing six bells. In 1886 it was re-roofed, reseated, a new vestry added, and several other improvements effected, costing £2,500. The 15th century rood screen was restored in 1877. The living is a vicarage, the gift of the Dean and Chapter of Windsor, and is valued at £200. A reredos has lately been placed, the panels representing four great missionary saints, SS Patrick, Augustine of Canterbury, Boniface and Columba, with a centre panel containing a replica of Raphael's Madonna and child

A Mission Chapel of the Good Shepherd, at Oreston, was restored, and new chancel added in 1889. There is a Wesleyan Chapel at Oreston, and a Bible Christian Chapel lately re-opened. Limestone and marble are got extensively in the parish. The Duke of Bedford is lord of the manor. Population in 1881 was 3,174, and in 1891 3,102. Here is a station on a branch of the L. & S. W. Railway from Plymouth, now carried on to Turnchapel; other near stations are at Marsh Mills, Billacombe, Elburton Cross, and Plympton. Steam ferries run every half hour from Oreston to Phœnix wharf, Plymouth.

HOOE is a separate ecclesiastical parish, taken out of Plymstock in 1855, and comprises the villages of Hooe, Turnchapel, Batten, Bovisand, and Staddon, and has a population of 1,364, including 400 soldiers, stationed at Staddon, Bovisand and Stamford forts. The living is a vicarage of £325 a year and house, in the gift of Keble College, Oxford. The church is dedicated to St. John, and consists of nave, chancel and south aisle and holds about 400 worshippers. There is a large National School adjoining the church.

PRIVATE RESIDENTS.

Alger John, Elburton
Annis Silas, churchwarden, Soloman lodge, Elburton
Belcher lieut-colonel J. W., M.D., Royal Army Medical Corps, Whitestock vil, Turnchapel
Bortwright Mrs Rachael, Plymstock
Bulteel Thomas, Mansion House, Radford
Charley Mrs Mary, Oreston
Clark Mrs Elizabeth, Russell house, Plymstock
Cochram E. P. West Hooe
Coleman Nicholas, Hooe
Collyns Rev Chas. B. B.A. vicarage Plymstock
Cooms William, Oreston
Cooper Mrs Mary, Plymstock
Davis Henry, Oreston
Ellis Philip N. Marine villa, Oreston
Evea Peter H. Pomphlet
Fitzgerald Maj. J. G. Fuzhatt hse, Plymstock
Fox George C. Turnchapel
Gascoyne Miss Jane, Elburton
Glasse Mrs, Billacombe villa
Grainger Mrs Sarah, Cliff cottage, Turnchapel
Hart J. W. F., Hooe
Hawker Mrs Helen, the Firs, Plymstock
Hicks Miss, Bellevue, Higher Hooe
Holton Mrs, Hillside, Plymstock
Hurrell James, Hooe
Inskip William, 8 Wellfield vls., Turnchapel
Jago W., Cliff cottage, Turnchapel
James Frederick, Elburton
Jefferson Chas. Wellfield villas, Turnchapel
Jones Capt. J. C. R.N. Russell House
Kingdon R. Wotton Down house, Plymstock
Knowles Mrs Mary, Oaklands, Plymstock
Little J., Thorn cottage, West Hooe
Longfield Wm. Digby (fleet-surgeon R.N.) St Anne's Hooe
Maddick James, Kerswill house, Hooe
Millman Roger, Dean school, Plymstock
Mills Henry, Wellfield villas, Turnchapel
Mitchell Thomas Harvey, Billacombe
Nelder Mrs M. J., Crichcoin house, Plymstock

Oxland George Hy. Turnchapel
Oxland Thomas, Oreston
Pascho John, The Hill, Turnchapel
Pascho Wm. Clovelly view, Turnchapel
Penter Jno. Marine villas, Oreston
Peter John, Park cott, Plymstock
Popplestone the Misses, Hooe house
Prout Miss Mary, Billacombe
Reynolds H. Chantry cottage, Hooe
Richards Capt Griffiths, The Retreat, Hooe
Rodney Frederick, Bovisand lodge
Scott S. Noy, D.P.H., L.R.C.P., M.R.C.S., Elmsleigh, Plymstock
Skilton Wm. Sunnyside
Staddon Roger, Kelly's cott, Turnchapel
Staddon Herbert, Turnchapel
Staddon Thos., Turnchapel
Stanlake Geo. R. Billacombe
Tapson Rev John James (vicar of St. John's Hooe) the vicarage, Turnchapel
Watts Henry, The Quay, Turnchapel
Watts Robert, Turnchapel
Watts Thomas, West Hooe
Walk T. Elburton
Willing Miss, Kerswill cottage, Hooe
Willis Mrs, Oreston
Williams John, Oreston
Yeo John Hart, Billacombe villa, Billacombe

1900 COMMERCIAL. 1900

Adams Mrs Mary, sweet shop, Oreston
Andrews Miss, news agent, West Hooe
Annis Mrs, gardener, Elburton
Annis R. *King Head inn*, Elburton
Ball A. E. watchmaker, West Hooe
Bayly R. and R. timber merchants, etc Oreston
Benmore Edwin Richard *Victoria inn*, Hooe
Bennett Chas. B. builder, etc. Turnchapel
Blatchford Chas. Thos. farmer, Goosewell
Body Hart, butcher, Elburton
Bradridge Albert J. station master, Bellacombe
British Battery Co., Ball A. E. manager
Brown Mrs Oph., *Borinqdon arms*, Turnchapel
Brown Chas. *New Inn*, Turnchapel
Brown J. H. baker and grocer, Oreston
Brown W. caretaker Wesleyan chapel, Oreston
Burgoyne Harry, carpenter, West Hooe
Burgoyne John, carpenter, Fanshawe cottages West Hooe
Burgoyne Saml. baker and grocer, West Hooe
Burlace Alfd. boat builder, Turnchapel
Canvin Amos, station master, Plymstock
Carter, Saml. grocer, Oreston
Cole Mrs A. M. postmistress and butcher, West Hooe
Cole Thomas, dairyman, Plymstock
Coleman Geo. blacksmith, Staddiscombe
Coleman Mrs Mary, shopkeeper, Turnchapel
Coleman Wm. blacksmith, Elburton
Coleman W. H. builder, Oreston
Cooms John, grocer, assistant overseer, Oreston
Cooms Thos. S. carpenter and undertaker, Oreston
Cooms Mrs Miriam, farmer, Millway farm, Oreston
Couch Wm. farmer, cab proprietor and carrier, Plymstock
Darton Hy. boat builder, Turnchapel
Darton Isaac Brace, boat builder, Mount Batten
Davis Henry S. master mariner, Oreston
Dawe Walter, farmer, Elburton
Dean Edward, bootmaker, Staddiscombe
Dean Wm. Hy. grocer, Turnchapel
Dean Wm. John, bootmaker and postmaster, Plymstock
Dodridge John, blacksmith, Plymstock
Dodridge Thos. blacksmith, Oreston
Dodridge Wm. contractor, Elburton
Edwards Elias, farmer, Oreston
Elford Henry, steamboat manager, Oreston
Ellis Mrs. haberdasher, Oreston
Ellis Philip, coal merchant, Oreston
Evans Hy. lighthouse keeper, Mount Batten
Evea Peter H. manager, Pomphlett quarries
Fairholme & Co. quarry owners, Hooe
Fletcher James, gardener, Turnchapel
Gascoyne Miss Jane, farmer, Elburton
Glasson Jas. H. baker and grocer, Plymstock
Glinn John, pilot, Turnchapel
Glinn John Haddy, pilot, Turnchapel

Gould E. Henry, farmer, Manor farm, Staddiscombe
Halteu J. shopkeeper, Turnchapel
Harper Thomas, school caretaker, Oreston
Harris Thos. tea gardens and farmer, Hooe
Hart Wm. Jno. F. coal merchant and lime quarries, West Hooe
Harvey Ed. & Richard, farmers, Coombe-Barton
Hendy Joseph, farmer, Elburton
Hendy Wm. Watts Harris, farmer, Elburton
Hendy John Bartlett, cowkeeper and blacksmith, Plymstock
Hewings Mrs Irene, *Royal Oak*, West Hooe
Higgins F. A. painter, Turnchapel
Higgins John, shoemaker, Turnchapel
Hine Frederick G. butcher, West Hooe
Hine George. *Castle inn*, Mount Batten
Hine John Henry, farmer, Pomphlet farm
Hine Philip, farmer, Court gate, Staddiscombe
Hine Philip B. jun. farmer, Turnchapel
Hobbs John, *Volunteer inn*, Elburton
Hockaday R. parish clerk, Plymstock
Holberton Wm. farmer, Elburton
Horn Reuben, market gardener and forage dealer, Plymstock
Jackson Joseph, bootmaker & grocer, Turnchapel
Jacobs Miss Elizabeth, general shopkeeper, Pomphlet
Jenkins R. farmer, Goosewell
Kelly John, baker, Turnchapel
Kelly Wm. Saml. ship builder, Mt Batten
Kingdon Richard, farmer, Down Horn farm, Plymstock
Lucas Wm. shipbuilder, Oreston
Maddick A. baker and grocer, Hooe
Marshall Wm. Hy. *Morley Arms*, innkeeper and coal merchant, Pomphlet
Mayes J. oilseller, Hooe
Mills Mrs, grocer, Elburton
Mills Mrs Jane Mary, private school, Turnchapel
Mitchell Wm. miller and farmer, Pomphlet
Moore Fredk. J. lime merchant, Elburton
Nichols Eli, builder and tea gardens, 8 Wellfield villas, Turnchapel
Northcott Brothers, market gardener, Home farm
Oats Jas. oil merchant, Turnchapel
Oborne Henry, baker, West Hooe
Oreston and Turnchapel Steamboat Company ltd. (S. Popplestone, sec ; Hy. Elford, manager)
Parson John, farmer, Elburton
Parsons Charles, carpenter, Marchant house, Plymstock
Parsons John, *Church house inn*, Plymstock
Passmore Miss Elizabeth, shopkeeper, Oreston
Pearce Thos. farmer, Ley port, Staddiscombe
PILE SAMUEL EDWARD, *King's Arms*, and ship chandler, Oreston
Pile Wm. sexton, Plymstock
Pridie John, baker and grocer, Oreston
Rapson R. baker, Staddiscombe
Reid Thos. butcher and grocer, Oreston
Rendle John, wheelwright, Plymstock
Roberts Hy. pier master, Turnchapel
Rowe Saml. bootmaker, Turnchapel
Rudd and Ellis, bakers, Oreston
Scott S. Noys Dr. surgeon (medical officer of health to Plympton St. Mary Rural District) Elmsleigh, Plymstock
Sherrell J. farmer, West Hooe
Skilton Hy. pilot, Turnchapel
Skilton Wm. pilot, Turnchapel
Smallridge Richard, gardener, Elburton
Sparrow and Co. quarry owners, Pomphlet and Billacombe
Spencer Robert, builder, Oreston
Spencer Thos. builder, Oreston
Staddon Thos. pilot, Turnchapel
Start W. manager to R. and R. Bayly, timb merchants, Oreston
Stentaford Oliver, quarry manager
Tapley Robert, carpenter and undertaker, Hooe
Taylor Jas. Jno. steamboat offices, Oreston
Vosper N. farmer, Wixenford farm, Plymstock
Wakeham E. farmer and butcher, Oreston
Watts James, farmer, Elburton
Westlake James, coal merchant, Turnchapel
Willcocks John, bootmaker, Plymstock
Willing Saml. grocer, the Row, Turnchapel, P.O.
Woodley George, *Shipwright's Arms*, Turnchapel
Wotton J. farmer, Court farm, Plymstock

Pomphlett Mill and Cottages

The Mill and cottages are viewed from the top of "New Hill", built when the railway was laid in 1898, which is now part of the main road to Oreston. Stamp's Bridge is in the far distance. The mill building is standing out from the cottages where the two people are walking. All these buildings are gone which overlooked Pomphlett Creek.

Shag Rock Marker

This metal frame and dome was made in the blacksmith's shop at the Breakwater Works sometime before the First World War. Frederick Rogers is at the top. Messrs. Brown, Oxland and Norsworthy(?) have been identified and the man in the suit is a Mr. Smith who was the foreman living in the Quarry house.

Breakwater Crew

Seen here in training for one of the many pre-First World War Sutton Harbour Regattas are Captain William Johns, Bill Harper, Harry Ellis, Charlie Jackson, Jack Dare, Joe Jackson, and Fred Rogers with others at Pomphlett creek. Note the lime kilns in the far background.

Plymstock Post Office

William Dean (1844–1924) was the village postmaster for forty-two years in the building shown on the right which is now a private house close to St. Mary's Church. He ran it with his wife Charity, Jenney with a shoemakers shop at the rear of the building.

Staddiscombe Post Office

In 1917 the post office and shoe-making business moved to a new house a short distance up the hill. The photograph below, taken about 1912, shows Mary Dean standing outside with a small child, Eleanor Rendle.

Amelia and Ernest Dean

They can be seen standing together outside the Staddiscombe post office in 1923. The bearded William Clatworthy, Amelia's brother, is looking out of the porch. He was the coachman at the Royal Hotel, Plymouth.

PRESENTED TO S. NOY SCOTT
MRCS - LRCP - DPH

The Parochial Church Council of Plymstock desire to record deep appreciation of the Service, Devotion, Love and Example in well-doing for the benefit of others, unfailingly given by Dr. Scott over a period of 54 years as friend, advisor and serving as Sidesman, Warden and Treasurer. It is regretted by all that Dr. and Mrs Scott have left Plymstock, but pray they may enjoy much happiness and long life. The following subscribe their names and many more would so desire —

Mrs I. Aldgate, Miss Ambrose, Mr. J. Anstey, Mrs. E. Anstey, Mrs. Ashford, Mrs. Adlam, A. M. Axworthy, Miss M. Bateman, A. Bennett, Mr. & Mrs Bishop, Miss M. Birch, Mr. & Mrs Boulter, Miss Boulter, Mrs Burgoyne, Mr. J. Bunker, F. Bunker, M. Bunker, A. Bunker, W. Bligh, Mr. & Mrs. Brendon, Mrs. Budge, A. Bryant, Mrs. Camp, Mr. & Mrs Canniford, Mr. & Mrs Caren, Nurse Carter, Mrs. E. Cattell, Mrs. Chapman, Mr. & Mrs. Comer, Miss Cooper, Mrs. J. Down, Mr. E. Down, S. Down, Mrs. E. Dean, Miss E. Doddridge, F. Edwards, S. Edwards, Mrs T. Ellis, Miss Eva, Mrs. Fox, Mr. & Mrs W. Frost, Mrs. M. Glinn, Col. H. G. Hawker, Miss. H. M. Hawker, E. Hine, D. Hendy, Mrs F. Harper, Mr. Frank Hendy, Mr. J. Hendy, Mrs. J. Holten, Mr. & Mrs. Hunt, Mr. & Mrs. Hay, Mr. & Mrs. Hine, Mr. W. G. Hackworthy, Mrs. S. Hammett, Miss Hendy, Mrs F. N. Hendy, Mr. E. Horn, Mr. & Mrs Hobbs, Comdr. Jones (C.H.P.), Mrs. Jones, Mrs F. Jackman, Mrs. M. James, Mr. & Mrs. Jackson, Mr. Lugar, Mr. & Mrs. Lang, E. Mitchell, Mr. & Mrs S. W. Mitchell, Mr. & Mrs S. Mitchell, Miss W. Mitchell, Mrs. Newby, Mr. & Mrs S. Nosworthy, N. Nosworthy, Mr. C. Nosworthy, Mrs. M. Oxland, Mrs. R. Pascho, Miss E. Peard, Mr. & Mrs. W. Payne, Miss. A. Payne, Mr. & Mrs W. Pile, Capt. & Mrs Polkinghorne, Mrs. M. Palmer, Mrs. C. D. Palmer, Mr. A. Penter, The Misses Penter, Mr. & Mrs Port, Mr. & Mrs Paige, Mr. W. Pearse, M. Pearse, Mr. A. Parsons, D. Parsons, Mr. & Mrs. C. Parsons, Miss Parsons, Miss B. Parsons, Mr. & Mrs J. Ryder, Mr. Reed, Miss. A. Reed, Miss K. Reed, Mrs. Renouf, Mrs. Rapson, Mr. & Mrs Revell, Miss Rogers, Mrs. A. Spencer, Mr. & Mrs G. Spencer, Miss Shanks, The Shirwills, Mrs. Stribling, Miss E. Spencer, Mrs. F. Start, Mr. & Mrs. F. Spencer, Mr. & Mrs. J. Spencer, Mrs. H. Spencer, Mr. F. Taylor, Mrs. F. H. Tope, Mrs. M. Tope, Tope, Mrs E. Tope, M. Tope, Mrs. M. Turner, Mr. & Mrs. Tallon, Mr. Vickory, Mr. Vickery, Mrs. Voysey, Mr. J. W. Williams, Rev. & Mrs. Wreford, Mr. & Mrs. Warne, Mr. G. Warley, Mr. G. Williams, Mr. & Mrs S. J. Wood, Mr. & Mrs Warley, Miss Warley, Miss B. Wills, M. Wills, Mr. John Wills, Mr. G. West, K. West, Mrs. White, Mrs. Weeks, M. Westlake, F. Westlake, Mr. H. Weston, F. Weston, B. Watts, E. Yearlings, C. P. C. Bligh.

Christmas 1925.

War Memorial Ground

This was given by W. S. Cooke, at Burrow Hill, at the end of the First World War which now also serves as the memorial to the 1939-45 war.

DR. S. NOY SCOTT.

PLYMPTON POSITION RESIGNED.

Plympton Guardians yesterday received with "deep regret" the resignation of Dr. S. Noy Scott from the position of Poor-law medical officer and public vaccinator, as from December 31.

Dr. Scott wrote that when the time for his resignation came he would have held the offices for 31 years. During the last few years the strain of excessive work during the war had made it necessary for him to lessen his work and responsibilities. "The long association I have had with many successive Boards of Guardians, and some of you for nearly the whole period, has been marked by such harmonies and pleasant features that I am sending in my resignation with much regret."

Moving the acceptance of the resignation Lieut. Abell and Mr. Davy paid tribute to the splendid manner in which Dr. Scott had carried out the duties of his offices.

A rather painful case of an ex-service man disabled in the war who had had his pension cut down to 8s. a week—his sole income to maintain a wife and two children—came before the Board, several members speaking indignantly of the manner in which some of these ex-service men were being forced to appeal for assistance to Guardians.—It was decided to bring the case to the notice of the Ministry of Pensions.

Presentation Certificate

As a mark of the high esteem held for Dr. Noy Scott this certificate was given to him, signed by many well wishers, at Christmas, 1925.

ELECTION 1906

Totnes Parliamentary Division.

PLYMSTOCK & WEMBURY PARISHES

Complimentary Dinner

TO

F. B. MILDMAY, Esq., M.P.

At the
Balfour Hall, Plymouth,

THURSDAY, 21st JUNE, 1906.

T. BULTEEL, Esq., J.P., Chairman
J. J. PASCHO, Hon. Secretary.

Eva's Cottages

These formerly stood on the north side of the main road approaching Laira Bridge from Plymstock and they normally housed workers in F. J. Moore's quarries. The photograph dates from the 1920s during which time Mr. and Mrs. Davis were one of the tenants. The cottages' name records Peter Halse Eva, manager for a Mr. Sparrow who owned the quarries before Mr. Moore moved out from Plymouth around 1896 and, until his death in 1924, was the principal quarry owner in the area.

Radford Castle

This building is very well known in the Plymstock locality and stands on part of the wall holding back a large head of water. This view dates from 1917 when it was the home of the Edwards. Later a Mr. and Mrs. T. H. Onion lived there. There were two white gates in the archway which were opened when members of the families living in Radford House passed this way.

Mr. J. Fairchild's Enterprise at Plymstock

A model bakery—the new premises of Mr. J. Fairchild's Reliance Bakery and General Stores—has been established in Plymstock.

This consists of an airy two-storied building behind the shop with the bakehouse, bread-store and garage on the ground floor, and the flour-loft above.

The bakehouse contains very modern equipment and the ideal amount of space and methods of ventilation.

The huge coke oven is one of the latest models made by Messrs. Collins, of Bristol, and a large space has been left by its side to allow for the installation of another oven if required.

Electric Dough Machine

An electric dough machine and one for cakes have also been installed; all the other processes being done by hand; three men having employment in the bakehouse.

Adjacent to this "ideal kitchen," the loaves are stored, on racks and trolleys, arranged so that air can penetrate through all the bread, in accordance with modern hygienic ideas.

Quantities of pastries and a variety of cakes, small and large, rich and plain, are made each day. Mr. Fairchild specializes in doughnuts which often travel as far as the Midlands and every day into the far reaching corners of the district they serve.

Curiously enough, the weather influences the sale of cakes, etc., a great deal. Muffins and doughnuts sell in abundance in the colder days, whereas the public favour the lighter "fancies" such as cream buns and Nelson squares in the summer.

"Farmhouse" Bread

Holidaymakers, and more especially Londoners, expect good confectionery, and the Reliance Bakery's "Farmhouse" Bread finds favour among them. It is in great demand locally. The men start delivering at 8 o'clock as the district covered comprises Oreston, Elburton, Radford, Dean's Cross, Billacombe, Pomphlett, Yealmpton, Newton, and Noss, Wembury, parts of Plympton, and of course, Plymstock.

Mr. Fairchild's enterprise in introducing such a necessary modern establishment into this rapidly growing area will be generally commended.

Mr. J. Fairchild's Enterprise, 1933

This was part of the heading given by a local newspaper to the opening of the Reliance Bakery and General Stores in Church Road in March, 1933. The article gives many particulars of this undertaking. The building is still in use but not as a bakery. Of recent years it sells clothes under "Carnabys" mainly for young people.

Plymstock Social Club, 1930

One of the many events for the club during this year was this charity football match at Dean Meadow. The team comprised of many age groups and was of a friendly nature. The exact occasion has not been recalled but Sam Kerswell, Graham Rodgman, Jack Bell, Alfie Martin, Ryder, MacDonald and Buckingham have been identified here.

Plymstock School, 1924

Pupils in standard V are assembled here in the school playground. Recognised among them are Cecil Doney, Lane, Alger, Sparkes, Reg Coleman, Norman Carter, Jumbo Edwards, Kathleen Ham, Dorothy Edwards, Honor Congdon, Iris Lawrence, Edith Hicks, Joyce Phillips, Marian Rowland, Faith Small, Winnie Pitts, Audrey Rickard, Elsie White, Jim Sparkes and Clifford Medland. The school then had about 150 pupils!

Goosewell School
School Children, about 1905

Back row: Jessie Doddridge, Alice Full, Olive Budge, Mary Dean, Freda Millamn, Annie James, M. Prowse, Davis, Annie Rapson. Middle row: Miss Gladys Bateman, teacher, Linda Griffiths, Mabel Jury, Lily Wyatt, Winnie Frost, Lorna Fowden, Marjorie Bateman, Gwen Gillard, Sarah Jury, Gladys Budge, Dora Full. Front row: Roger Griffiths, Gillard, Dorothy Budge, May Lavers, Nora Bateman, Alberta Axworthy, Beatrice Fowden, Dorothy Ellis, Florrie Doddridge, Rose Ellis and Miss Cooper, headmistress. The boy holding the slate is Roy Callard.

Civil War Cannon (1640s)

A reminder of the local battles which occurred in the area is this weather-worn cannon lying close to the war memorial on Burrow Hill. There were four cannon balls alongside it years ago but these have long disappeared.

Goosewell Almshouses

A once familiar sight at the bottom of Goosewell Hill they were built at the expense of Sir Christopher Harris, of Radford House, for the benefit of five poor people. They were demolished in the 1960s to make way for the present buildings.

Bill Budge

Seen here proudly standing with his grand daughter, Hilma Glinn. They lived in 4 Goosewell Terrace before and during the First World War.

Plymstock Railway Station about 1900

This served passengers for the Yealmpton line: a G.W.R. steam train is coming into the platform on the left and the L.S.W.R. line to Oreston and Turnchapel is to the right. It had only been opened a few years before this view was taken. The station was damaged during the war, passenger trains stopped running in 1947 and freight trains ceased in 1960.

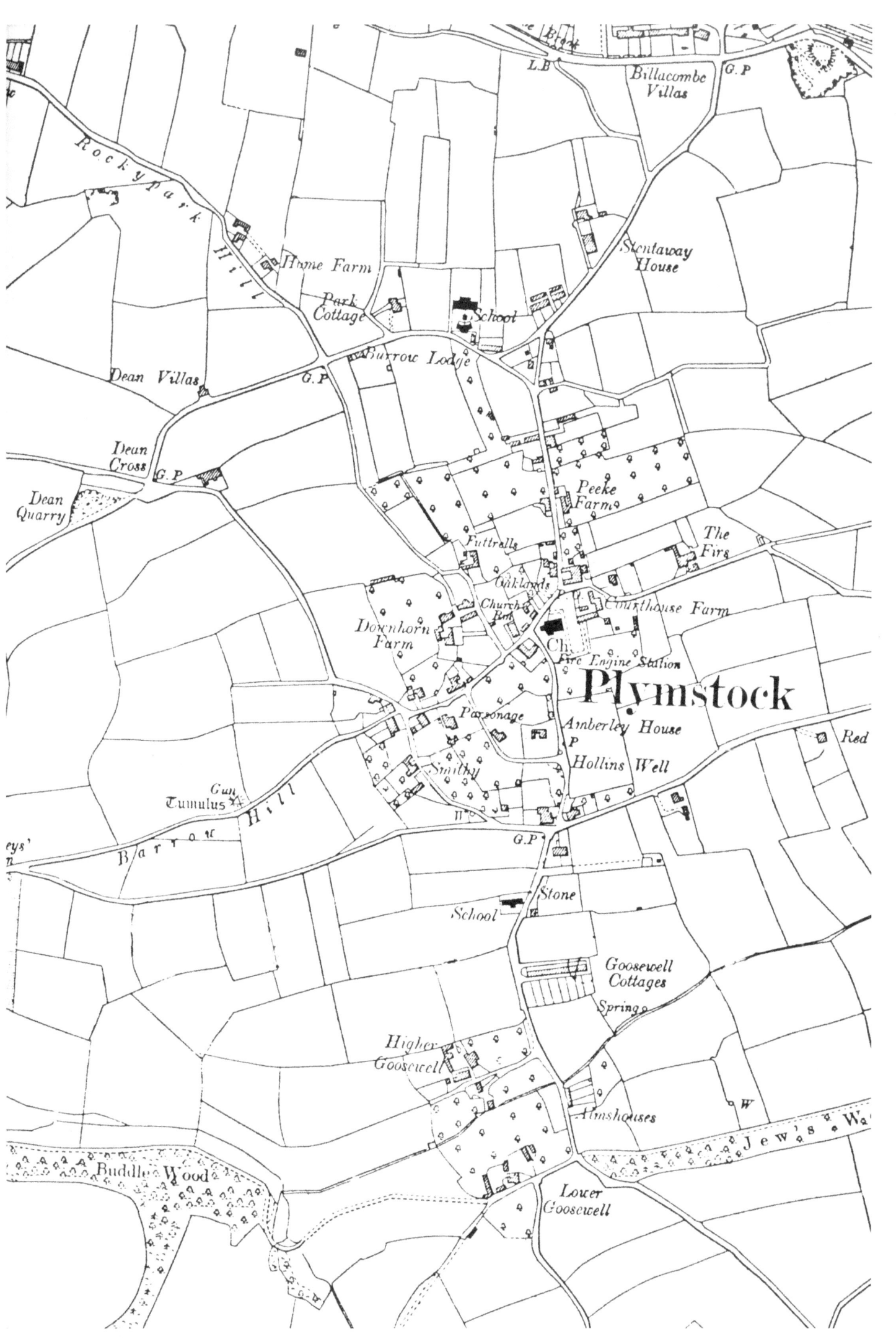

Home Farm, Plymstock, 1951

A last reminder of this well known farm then worked by F. Rowland a few weeks before it was cleared for the R.A.F. private houses. He worked it from 1934; C. W. Rowland was there from 1920 and J. H. Rowland from 1911. It comprised of about 50 acres of land mainly devoted to market gardening, there were five cows producing milk for the Dean Cross dairy which opened in 1928.

Councillor H. J. Rowland

Lending a hand at harvest time on Home Farm in 1930, Mr. Rowland was then active in local affairs following a successful career in market gardening. Dunstone Woods are in the background.

"Lion" and "Tiger" in 1950

These two stalwarts are taking a well earned rest after a day's ploughing on the market garden. Other duties were delivering to shops in Plymouth, collecting loads of dung each day from the Dockyard and local deliveries. They were handled by Bert Wood who lives at Homeleigh Cottages and were sold at Plympton cattle market when the land was sold.

Goodbye to Home Farm in 1951!

A chapter is closing on a scene in Plymstock known for hundreds of years. Here W. Davis and Son is starting to remove a roof in readiness for the demolition of the farm buildings. This was in preparation for new building developments which make up part of the R.A.F. housing estate.

Harvesting in 1933

A moment of happy relaxation on Home Farm during the annual harvest, this time in 1932. Charles Rowland is helped by family and friends but who would have then thought that these scenes were numbered?

Plymstock Farmer, 1933

Solid limestone walls, stout footwear, free range chickens are just three points of this photograph showing Charles Rowland at one of his many daily jobs. There were then about twelve pigs, various poultry, cows and horses and the crops were of peas, beans, broccoli, etc.

William Clatworthy, coachman, Royal Hotel, Plymouth

These two photographs show William in attendance at a Plymouth station with the Hotel's horse and coach and then the later modern carrier van. Taken at the time of the First World War this kind of work gave employment to many local men.

Amelia Dean, Postmistress

Here sitting in the chair presented on her retirement after twenty-five years at Staddiscombe. The inhabitants of the village, Down Thomas and Bovisand all contributed to its purchase.

Ernest Dean, Postmaster

Staddiscombe's postmaster for twenty-five years, Ernest (1857–1926), first worked with William Dean making and repairing boots and shoes in the workshop behind Plymstock's post office. He married Amelia, working in service at Oaklands, then moved to Staddiscombe where he both ran the post office and undertook shoemaking.

Two Bridges

These were once very familiar sights: the upper bridge at Stamp's Corner, Pomphlett, carried the trains to Oreston and Turnchapel and the lower one traffic to and from Plymouth over the Laira. The limestone rail bridge went in the 1960's having seen service since just before 1900. The cast iron bridge is not so busy as its modern successor seen here in February, 1930, with a solitary city bus making its way out to Plymstock. Note the sharp turn in the road.

The Laira Bridge, 1829

This well known engraving shows the iron ornamented structure with its toll house, to the left, two years after it was opened. The tolls were lifted in 1924 and the bridge replaced by the present one in 1961. It was Plymouth's first major bridge built by James M. Rendel, for the Earl of Morley, at a cost of £10,000.

In the News

Yesterday's newspapers are a great source of interesting and often amusing local information. The style of reporting has changed but events still take place. Here three reports give details of the Empire Day celebrations in 1922, the great blizzard in 1891 and the problems of an unsatisfactory water supply as recorded in the *Western Morning News* of 1895.

PARISH AND DISTRICT COUNCILS.

PLYMSTOCK.
UNSATISFACTORY WATER SUPPLY.

Plymstock Parish Council met last evening, Dr. S. Noy-Scott presiding.—The Finance Committee reported that the scale of charges as presented by Mr. Cleverton, returning officer, had again received their careful attention. In reply to a communication from the clerk, Mr. Cleverton had allowed £2 2s. on the charge for presiding officers. The charges for voting compartments was made in accordance with the scale, and though considered excessive they did not see in what way the Council had power to reduce them.—The Clerk read a letter from Mr. H. Michelmore, clerk to the County Council, in reference to the charge of the voting compartments. Mr. Michelmore wrote that in the absence of vouchers relating to this item, he was unable to say whether the charge was correct or not, but it appeared to him to be a very high charge indeed.—The report was adopted, on the motion of Mr. Lewarn, seconded by Mr. Evea.— Mr. Widdecombe moved that Mr. Cleverton's charges be again referred to the consideration of the Finance Committee.—Mr. Michelmore seconded.—Mr. Lewarn moved as an amendment, "That if Mr. Cleverton reduced the charge of returning officers to one-half, as done to the presiding officer, the Finance Committee be empowered to pay the account."—The amendment was carried, seven voting for it and two against. The Chairman stated that the water supply at Plymstock was utterly inadequate. In the village of Pomphlett the water was stated to be impure, and all impure water liable to cause disease. Turnchapel and Oreston they ought to to have water sufficient to keep the sewers absolutely clean. Flushing was required more often. The people at the higher end of Pomphlett had to go Eberton to get water. There had been two schemes proposed for the supply of water. One was to bring water from Plymouth for the whole of the district, and the other to take the water from Plympton. Personally, if they had to go to either place, Plympton would be the more profitable scheme, but he was very much in favour, if possible, of getting the water in their own parish. (Hear, hear.) He thought, at any rate, they should seek water in Plymstock, and if that failed then they must go elsewhere. He proposed (1.) "That the water supply of the various villages in the parish of Plymstock, is insufficient in quality and very badly distributed"; (2) "There is urgent necessity for improving the same"; and (3) "That the District Council be asked to allow the Parish Council to co-operate with them in their duty to provide the parish of Plymstock with a pure and sufficient supply of water, and that the matter be taken in hand at once."—Mr. Couch seconded, and it was carried unanimously.—The General Purposes Committee reported that they had appointed the following as a committee to formulate a scheme for the better supply of water at Turnchapel, Pomphlett, and Oreston :—Dr. S. N. Scott, and Messrs. Evea, Lewarn, Couch, and Williams.— The Duke of Bedford's agent wrote offering to comply with the provisions of the Parish Councils Act, and to transfer to the Council his field allotments in Plymstock on a yearly tenancy on terms to be agreed upon between his Grace and the Parish Council.—On the motion of Mr. Widdicombe, seconded by Mr. Williams, the letter was allowed to stand over until applications had been made for allotments.— Mr. BATEMAN moved, "That notices be posted that the Parish Council would be prepared to receive written applications for allotments; and that working men should state the quantity of land required (pasture or arable), and that a committee of five be appointed to draw up and report what land was available and rules for the working of allotments."—Carried.

PLYMSTOCK

EMPIRE DAY CELEBRATION

On Wednesday, May 24th, the usual Empire Day celebrations were held at the senior school. Lessons were given on Empire subjects to the children, after which they assembled in the playground.

The chair was taken by Comdr. C. H. P. Jones, the Chairman of the School Managers, who opened the proceedings by briefly addressing the children on the origin and aim of "Empire Day." This was followed by the hoisting of the Union Jack, which was saluted by the assembled children, who then gave three hearty cheers for the King.

The children then rendered Kipling's "Children's Song," and this was followed by an excellent address to the children by Dr. S. Noy Scott.

This was followed by a short patriotic sketch in which Britannia (Edith Coleman), Patriotism (Leah Bunker), and Discontent (Phyllis Tope) took part, assisted by eight dancing maidens.

The annual prize distribution then took place, the prizes being distributed by Mrs. Leatham, of Stentaway, Plymstock. Comdr. Jones also presented the medals given to the best all-round boy and girl, elected by their fellow scholars. The boy's medal, given by Comdr. Jones, was won by Frank Bate, and the girl's medal, presented by Capt. G. Clow, was won by Vera Adams.

The singing of the National Anthem by the school children and the assembled parents brought a successful celebration to an end.

After the close the parents and other visitors were invited to see an exhibition of work done by the scholars during the course of their school work.

PLYMSTOCK
APRIL, 1891.

THE terrific storm which commenced on Monday morning, March 9th, and continued without interruption all through that fearful Monday night, the wind blowing with hurricane force right on through the whole of Tuesday, and not abating in violence till the Wednesday morning,—with an excessively heavy fall of snow, the drifts in many places being from six to ten feet deep, and even worse—sadly interfered with our pre-arranged system of Lenten Services. Never, perhaps, will the writer of these lines forget his journey up from Oreston in the teeth of the storm when its fury was about at its height, at 8 to 8-30 on that Monday night. The force of the wind, and the heavily falling snow were so blinding that it was impossible to face them directly, and all he could do was to sidle along under such shelter as the low stone walls afforded, sometimes going backwards altogether, and quite at a loss as to whereabouts he was on the road. More than once the exhaustion produced by battling with the hurricane prompted the idea of lying down and giving up in despair, but by God's mercy he was able to keep pounding on until Dean Cross was reached, and a few minutes' hospitable shelter was given him by good old Mrs. Milman at the School Cottage. Like hundreds of other poor belated travellers, never was he so thankful to reach home as on that night, and reaching home meant not venturing out again till Wednesday morning. The effects of the storm in our parish, and especially in our home village, it is almost impossible to adequately describe ; house roofs stripped piecemeal, windows broken by falling slates, hundreds of fine stout elms and beeches, and other trees levelled —the churchyard suffering somewhat severely. For some days vehicular traffic was entirely interrupted, and it was with the greatest difficulty that pedestrians could make their way from one part of the parish to another. The immediate effects of the storm made it necessary to suspend all Church Services that week ; the state of the roads even on the following Sunday, by reason of the deep snowdrifts and fallen trees (in Furzhatt-lane, by Helland's Well, the huge trunks were lying right across, piled one above another, forming a kind of barricade), making it a matter of impossibility for some parishioners, and a very difficult task for any, to reach the Parish Church.

Radford Mansion, demolished 1935-37

Plymstock's largest house, a mansion, made famous with its links with Drake and Raleigh was the home of the Radford family, the Harris's and finally the Bulteels. Bought by the Mitchells around 1917 it remained largely empty until Harold Triggs with six men gained the contract for demolishing it and putting up for sale lead, timber, stone, etc.

An Outing to Cheddar in 1924

All smiles for the start of this open topped char-a-banc outing from Pomphlett Chapel in 1924. Among those here are Mr. and Mrs. Fred Tall, Miss Olive Morrish, Mr. Bramwell, Mrs. Wavish, Winnie Mitchell and Katherine Rowland. It is thought that this photograph was taken close to the chapel. Note the car which is believed to have been Mr. Kirby's, the notice on the wall and sign on the hard-tyred vehicle.

Anniversary Day, 1957

Scholars of the Pomphlett Sunday School are grouped here smiling for the occasion not too many years ago. Among those recognized are Rosemary Goodman, Diane Rowe, Rosemary Hendy, Sheila Holmes, Janice Coniam and Catherine Dalley with others.

Goosewell School, about 1897

These details were recorded by Mrs. Mary Glinn (née Dean) of Liskeard in 1982. From back: Miss Kate Dean, teacher, Sarah Watts, Lizzie Holberton, two Ellis children, Elsie Sherrill, Ida Sherrill, Lily Alger, Nellie Dean. Then Watts, Flossie Lavers, Emily Rowe, Eva Doddridge, Jenny Doddridge, Eveline Ball, Margaret Shillabeer, Celia Doddridge, Polly Watts, Sarah Watts, Mary Dean, George Ball, Emily Lavers, Ethel Dean, Elsie Frost, Rowland Sherrill, Harry Dean and George Lavers with the headmistress, Miss Cooper, holding Winnie Frost.

Goosewell School about 1924

Three decades later and the faces change to Roger Sims, Bill Eastley, Ron Glinn, Cyril Carter, Ivor Body, Miss Mardon, teacher, Eileen MacGregor, Ruby MacGregor, Ethel Beer, Arthur Staddon, Sid Hicks, Griffiths, Eric Warley, Tony Bateman, Ivor Avent and Bertie Townsend with others unidentified.

Plymstock Scouts

The annual camp was held for many years at Revelstoke and here a group are seen enjoying themselves during the 1930 visit. The scoutmaster was Mr. A. Pearn, his assistant Mr. Wood. Recognised are Fred Rowland, Terence Roname, Paul Rogers, Jack Shillabeer with other local lads and the pet dog.

BILLACOMBE AND DISTRICT ALLOTMENT
AND GARDEN ASSOCIATION
& PLYMSTOCK CIVIL DEFENCE

SCHEDULE

A VICTORY GARDEN SHOW

AT THE

PLYMSTOCK SENIOR SCHOOL

ON 11TH SEPTEMBER, 1943

IN AID OF THE

RED CROSS

THE SHOW WILL BE OPENED AT 2 p.m. BY

MRS. LORNE SAYERS

Chairman :
Mr. H. W. Kitt.

Hon. Sec :
Mr. E. Latham.

Hon. Treasurer :
Mr. W. F. Avery.

Judges :
Mr. R. J. Welsh. Mrs. M. Gibson.

Auctioneer :
Capt. C. F. Viner.

ENTRIES must be in by WEDNESDAY, 8th SEPTEMBER, and should be sent to the Secretary on entry forms provided.

ADMISSION.

From 2 p.m. to 4 p.m.   ADULTS 1/-   CHILDREN 6d.

AFTER 4 p.m.   ADULTS 6d.   CHILDREN 3d.

CLARKE, DOBLE & CO., LTD., PRINTERS, PLYMOUTH.

Plymstock Imps Football Club, 1927–28

Seen here in the Devon Minor League are D. Paul, J. Pearse, S. Taylor, J. Smith, T. Fansom, C. Pearse, C. Shepherd, H. Morgan (captain), J. Sparkes, A. Shepherd, P. Dolton, T. Corel, H. Couling and J. Hall.

Goosewell School Class in 1927

Four rows of boys and girls make up this group for the photographer sometime during 1927. Recognised here are Bill Eastley, Horton, Ivor Avent, Cyril Carter, Eric Warley, Anniss, Sid Hicks, Ron Glinn, Joan Renouf, Doris Stevenson, Ethel Beer, Beryl Westlake, Mary Staddon with others.

Radford "Duck Ponds"

These three photographs of Radford Lake were taken in 1919 when they were still part of the private Radford estate. A public footpath gave access down to Hooe Lake but the area was not as open as it is today. Affectionately known as the *Duck Ponds* the head of water was controlled by a sluice gate close to the castle-like building below these views.

St. Keverne's Quay

The present ruins on the edge of the water are seen here in their habitable state complete with a boathouse and strong protecting wall. Mr. and Mrs. Southern lived here for many years while he worked as a gardener at Hooe Manor. The buildings were part of the Radford estate and presumably date from the time when the lake was dammed.

The Armoury

The higher of the two buildings was known as *The Armoury* although any connection with arms has not been established. The lake is viewed from its higher end showing the once very delightful setting with a surrounding belt of mature trees. Many of these have gone but the locality still has a rural atmosphere about it and is very popular with local walkers.

Plymstock Parish Council in 1953

Posed for the Queen's coronation year are W. Baker, J. T. Pascho, S. C. Damerell, N. J. R. Carter, R. C. Loxley, W. A. G. Mitchell, Rev. R. G. Ball, F. C. Rowland, S. E. Kerswell, T. E. M. Savery, J. Finnigan, A. E. Townsend (vice-chairman), E. J. Hicks (chairman), L. W. W. Pettitt (clerk), G. R. Coleman.

County and Rural District Councillors (Plymstock parish) 1953

F. H. West, S. E. Kerswell, W. A. G. Mitchell, T. E. M. Savery, R. T. May, T. B. Goodsir, Mrs. R. Mitchell.

Arthur L. Clamp – the man behind the books

Arthur Leslie Clamp was a man of boundless energy with a passion for helping others, particularly through his love of history. A printer by trade, he started his career in a printing company before moving his family from Exeter to Plymouth to teach at the Plymouth College of Art and Design, where he eventually became the Head of the Printing Department.

Arthur with his five children.

A Devoted Family Man

Despite his love of teaching, Arthur prioritised his family, always making it home by 5:30pm for tea. He and his wife, Rosemary, raised five children: Susan, Angela, Elizabeth, David, and Steven. Arthur would often combine his love of family and history by taking his children on Sunday walks, encouraging them to appreciate historical monuments by taking photos or making crayon rubbings of gravestones for his books. The family home at 203 Elburton Road was a hub of activity, with a large garden, featuring a two-storey fort and a makeshift swimming pool.

A Lifelong Learner and Adventurer

Arthur's thirst for knowledge extended beyond history to a deep curiosity about the world. He was passionate about exploring different cultures, traditions, and cuisines, often taking advantage of his long summer holidays as a teacher to travel to places like India, Russia, South America, the middle east and the USA, sometimes bringing one of his children along. This adventurous spirit even influenced his home life, as seen by the short-lived family tradition of steam-cooking vegetables after a trip to Iceland.

History is a prominent feature of family days out

Community and Philanthropic Spirit

His commitment to serving others was evident in his long-standing involvement with the Elburton Methodist Church. He was the Sunday School Superintendent for over 15 years and served as the editor of the wider church's monthly newsletter, "The Link," for a similar duration. After Rosemary's very sad passing, Arthur later remarried and, following a chance encounter with a professor from India, established a connection with a missionary school in Chennai. Together with his new wife, Christine, he co-founded a "Sponsor a Child's Education" program that continues to this day.

*Pictured left – The cover of 'The Link' complete
with hand drawn sketches of each church by Angela
Below right – Arthur Clamp promoting his latest book
Below left – Arthur at home with his first wife, Rosemary
Below centre – Arthur on holiday with his second wife, Christine*

A Legacy of Learning and Positivity

Arthur's greatest passion was history, which he brought to life through tireless research, documentation, and the many books he authored. He was driven by a need to "never be stuck in a rut," constantly seeking new experiences, meeting new people, and expanding his knowledge. With a positive attitude and a great sense of humour, he was always ready to help others, leaving a lasting impact on his family and community. His children, Susan, Angela, Elizabeth, David, and Steven, remember him with love and gratitude.

David Clamp, 2025

A Legacy of Local History

Below is the story of how Arthur L Clamp began writing books, in his own words, drafted shortly before he passed away in 2001. I have only made minor alterations to this text, correcting grammatical errors that he did not survive to correct himself. When I first discovered this text, I was shocked to see my name mentioned. It seems that, unbeknownst to me, I shared my first PC with him. I suspect he used it during the day when I was at school, although I do have one memory of sitting with him and showing him how it worked. It has been a pleasure to pick up where he left off and see his books republished and redistributed, and to know that I was part of the story, even back then. It was also fascinating to discover that his pricing structure matches the way I have tried to price the books, with a third going to local sellers and the rest covering printing costs with a little left over for my expenses.

I am his eldest grandson, and it is a privilege to curate his legacy, which we are calling 'The Clamp Collection'. The very last line of the text originally reads "The following pages list all the titles." Sadly, that page is missing and we have no record of all the books he published and knowing that some of those were researched by other authors makes the process of finding them even harder. I look forward to one day completing the collection and seeing them all available again. And maybe, one day, I'll even start writing my own to add to the series. For now, here is his story in his own words.

Steven Gibson, 2025

Writing and Publishing Booklets on Local Topics and Areas

I started this interest in either 1968 or 1969 when living in Woodford. I had by these dates established the Department of Printing and I think I must have been looking for something different to do. The first titles were of A5 size proofed from type set at Clarke, Doble and Brendon, Ltd., Plymouth printers, and then made up into pages and printed at Sawtell and Neilson, Ltd., Totnes.

Then began a slow process of getting them out to shops, etc. which proved to be more time consuming and difficult than actually researching, writing and getting the books into print. However, I persisted and opened a business account with Barclays Bank on the Broadway. I was advised to give it a title so I called it "Westway Publications". There came along another problem, one of storage of paper and finished books which was solved when the family moved to Elburton in 1970.

I changed the printer to Penwell, Ltd., Callington, Cornwall, as he was then just setting up himself and his prices seemed very reasonable. I did not get any of the printers to make up the complete books. I hand folded the flat printed sheets, stitched the books on a small manual table stitcher and trimmed them in a small hand turned guillotine which I bought from someone in Penzance for £40. It was brought up in a van.

The trouble and time going to and fro to Callington was too much so I transferred the printing to PDS Printers, Prince Rock, Plymouth, and I have been with them ever since. Now they are at Plympton which is easy to reach and they fold the flat sheets which was turning out to be a long chore which only saved a small part of the printing costs.

All my first titles were written by myself. I took the photographs and developed them in the loft of the house, the type was set by now on a computer situated in the house at Elburton from which I had collected photographic lengths of text to cut up and law down as pages.

At some point I decided that I would do my own film processing of lith film so I bought a large second hand process camera from Kingsbridge and learnt through trial and error to make line negatives of the text and halftone negatives of the illustrations which proved more difficult than I anticipated. The main problem was trying to keep the developer in the large dish at the correct temperature as any change would affect the developing time. I replaced this old camera with a brand new one bought from Croydon, Surrey, costing £900. This has turned out to be a great asset cutting out an expensive part of the printer's costs and one crucial aspect of the work which I could control.

By the middle 1970s there were many outlets I had contacted in Plymouth, up to Dartmoor, Exeter, around to Torbay, Totnes, Dartmouth and the South Hams. The market for local books was much greater than I had first thought and through getting to know many local people undertaking research themselves had the chance to help and make up books for other people who had in most instances, got together a collection of photographs with some text in a rather muddled way. Through my experience in print I was able to shape up their work and get it into print and in every case I had to pay the printer and let the person have the royalties. In the majority of titles produced in this manner this was another way of producing titles and it did give some profit to my work. However, I must say that in a few cases I lost out by either the other person getting the numbers wrong, not returning any monies from stock I delivered or they thought that more of their books should have been sold.

The print run was usually 1,000 copies and from time to time I have had reprints of 250 copies. It took about ten years to clear the first print run so I always had large stocks in the garage, workshop, etc. The numbers sold during the early years was about 7,000 copies a year increasing to around 9,000 copies and for the whole of the enterprise about 500,000 have been sold. The booklets have become part of the local scene and many people collect them, shops regularly order copies and I go around certain areas month by month restocking or replacing titles as necessary.

During the past year or so I have started setting the text on a Packard Bell PC, something which I should have done some years back. I share it with Steven Gibson, my grandson. There appears to be no end to the market for local books, but I could not earn a regular income because of the long time it takes to sell stock.

However, now exceeding 100 titles made up mainly of A4 twenty-four page booklets, some folded guides, with selling prices set with a third going to the shop which is the trade custom, the original idea has been quite successful and could go on for ever.

Apart from monetary benefits, however spasmodically these might be, I have learnt a lot myself, met many interesting people and have become part of the local scene with requests to give talks and to advise people about getting into print.

Arthur L Clamp, 2001

This newspaper article, published by the Evening Herald on 17th August 2001, forms a good record of his life. Just as he encourages us to learn more about local history, we encourage you to learn a little about him. For that reason, we have included these pages at the back of all the most recently republished books, in honour of his memory and recognition of his contribution to the community.

www.ingramcontent.com/pod-product-compliance
Lightning Source LLC
Chambersburg PA
CBHW061407070526
44584CB00031B/4185